ETLING STRING CLASS METHC
STUDENT PROGRESS Cl

MW01153482

NAME _____   TEACHER _____

	PAGE	ASSIGNED Teacher	GRADE (OK) Teacher
LESSON #37	3		
LESSON #38	4		
LESSON #39	5		
LESSON #40	6,7		
LESSON #41	8,9		
LESSON #42	10		
LESSON #43	11		
LESSON #44	12		
LESSON #45	13		
LESSON #46	14,15		
LESSON #47	16		
LESSON #48	17		

	PAGE	ASSIGNED Teacher	GRADE (OK) Teacher
LESSON #49	18		
LESSON #50	19		
LESSON #51	20		
LESSON #52	21		
LESSON #53	22		
LESSON #54	23		
LESSON #55	24,25		
LESSON #56	26		
LESSON #57	27		
LESSON #58	28,29		
LESSON #59	30		
LESSON #60	31,32		

Alfred

Highland Etling
A Division of Alfred Publishing Co., Inc.

THE SCALE OF D MAJOR

(Review from Book 1)

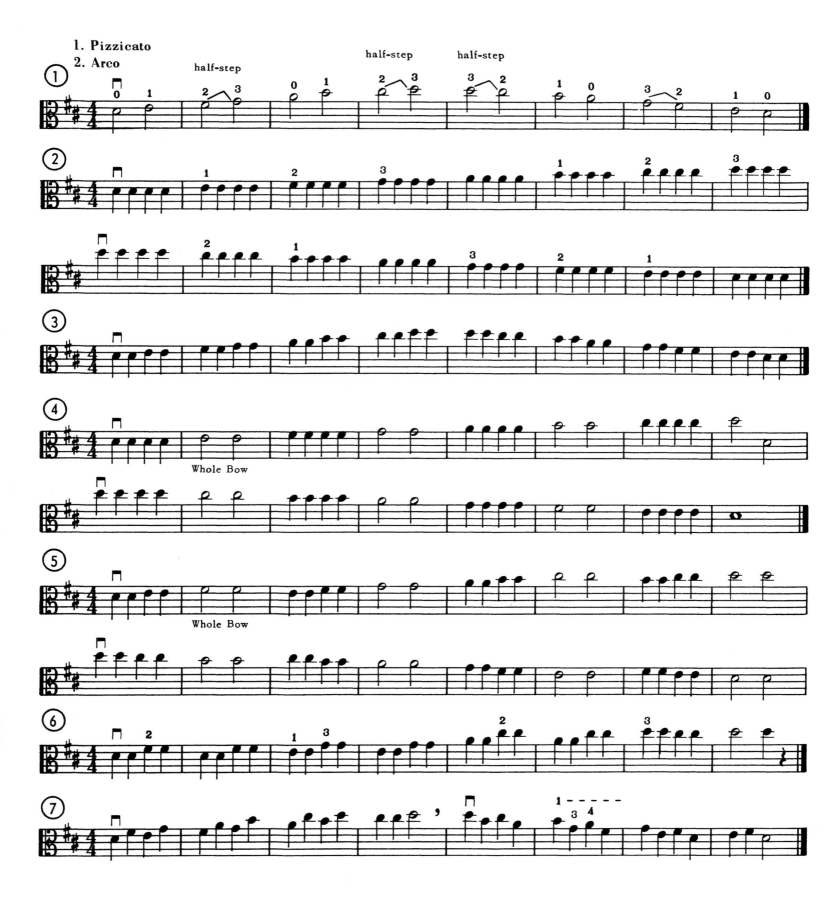

LONG, LONG AGO

LESSON #37

arr. by Forest R. Etling

Variation

THEME AND VARIATIONS

arr. by Forest R. Etling

LESSON #38

Spiccato Variant

simile

Slur Variant

Sixteenth Note Variant

Triplet Variant

C♮ ON THE A STRING

(Notice that there is no
C♯ in the key signature,
just the F♯)

(Test)

(accidental)

LESSON #41

F♯ ON THE C STRING

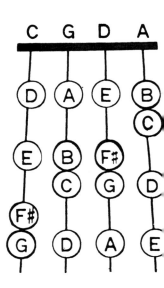

LEARN: The Key of G

A New Finger Pattern

①

2   **H 3**   (half-step)

(Notice that there is
only one sharp in the
key signature — F♯)

②

2   **H 3**   **1**

③

(half-step)

④

The G Scale

⑤

0   **1**   **2**   (half-step)   **3**   **1**   **2**   **H 3**   (half-step)   **4**

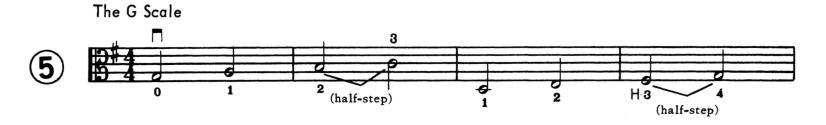

4   **3**   **2**   **1**   **3**

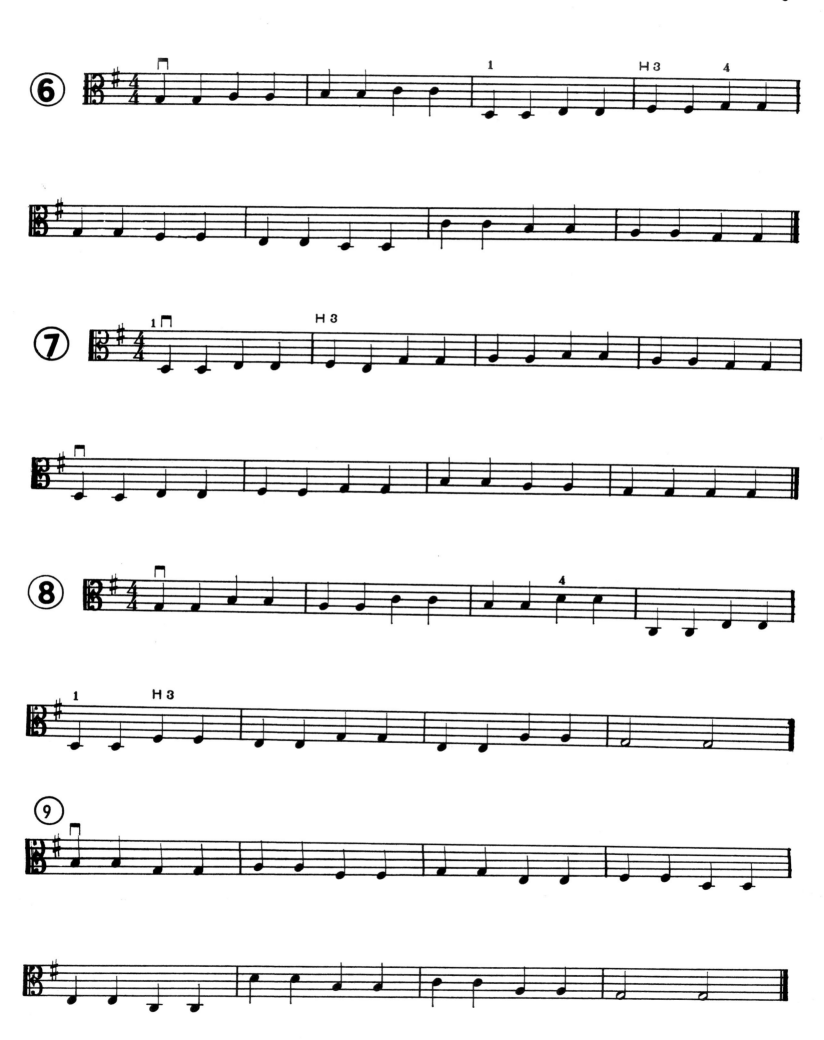

THE SCALE OF G MAJOR

DOUBLE-STOPS

MELODY

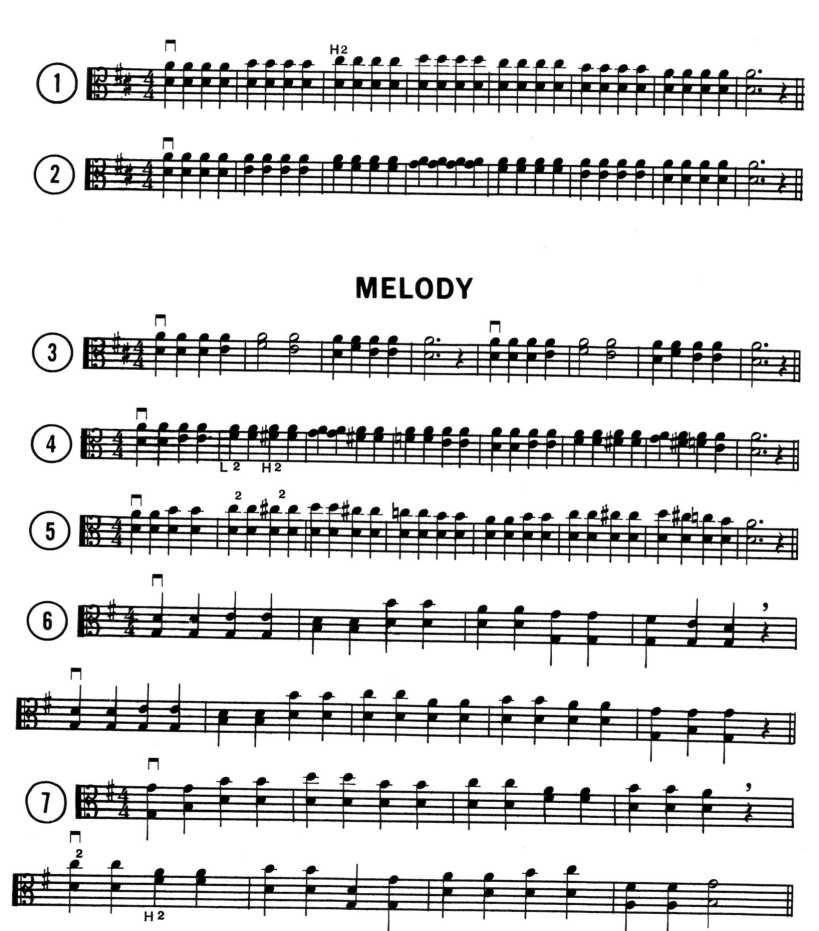

LESSON #44

SCHOOL MARCH

Hohmann—Forest R. Etling

IN THE COUNTRY

Hohmann—Forest R. Etling

COUNTING STUDY

Hohmann—Forest R. Etling

A CHALLENGE

Hohmann—Forest R. Etling

F♮ ON THE D STRING

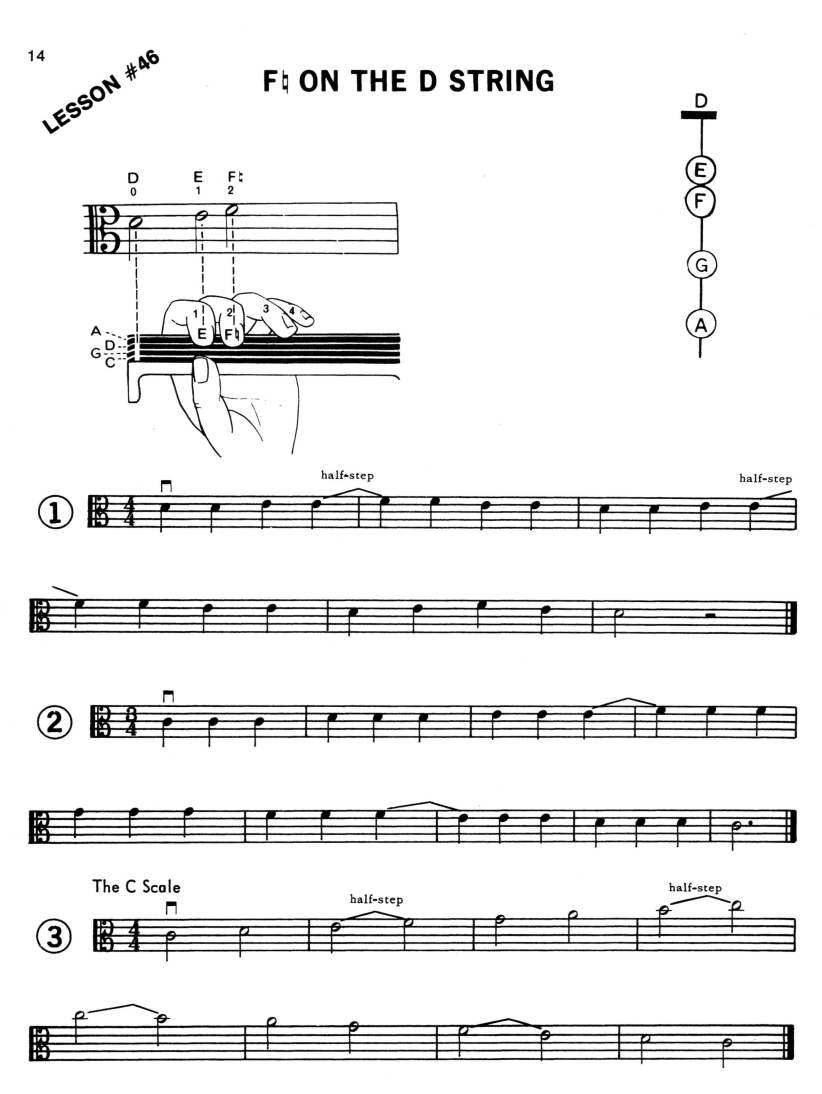

① half-step   half-step

②

The C Scale

③ half-step   half-step

LESSON #47

F♮ ON THE C STRING

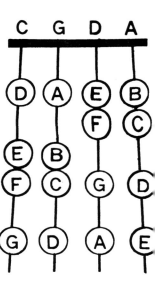

LEARN: The Key of C

① 2   ♯ H 3   (half-step)

② (Notice that there are NO
sharps in the key signature)

③ 0   1

The C Scale

④ 0   1   2   3   2

3   3   2   1

⑤   L 2

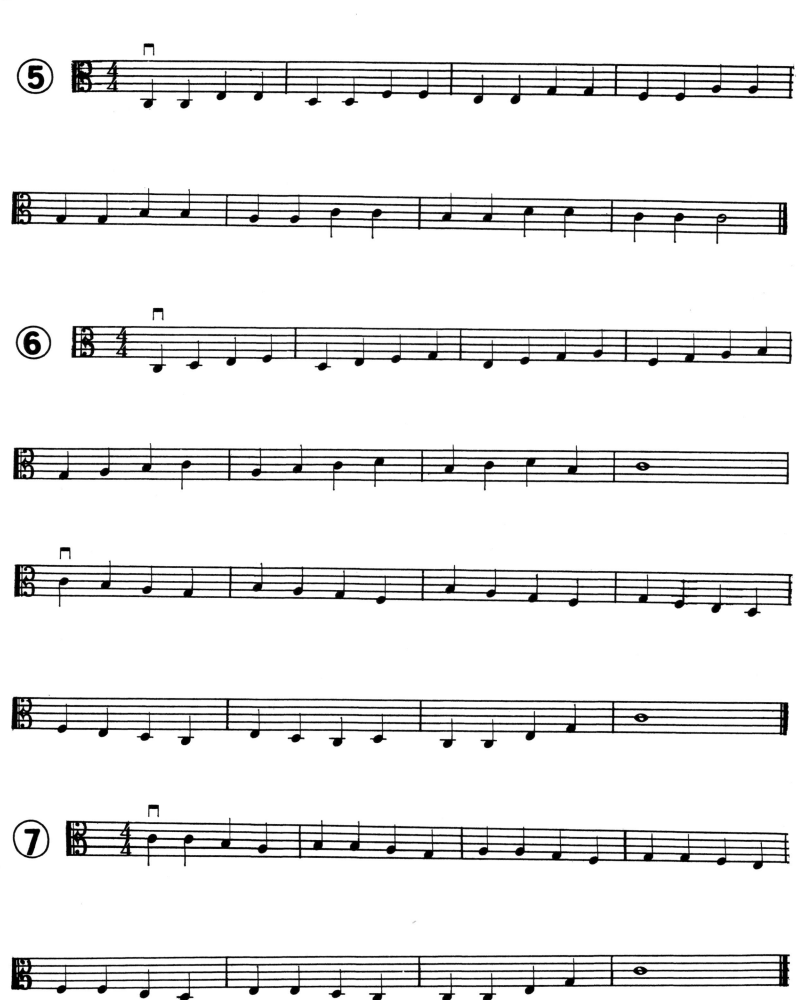

18

LESSON #49

STUDY

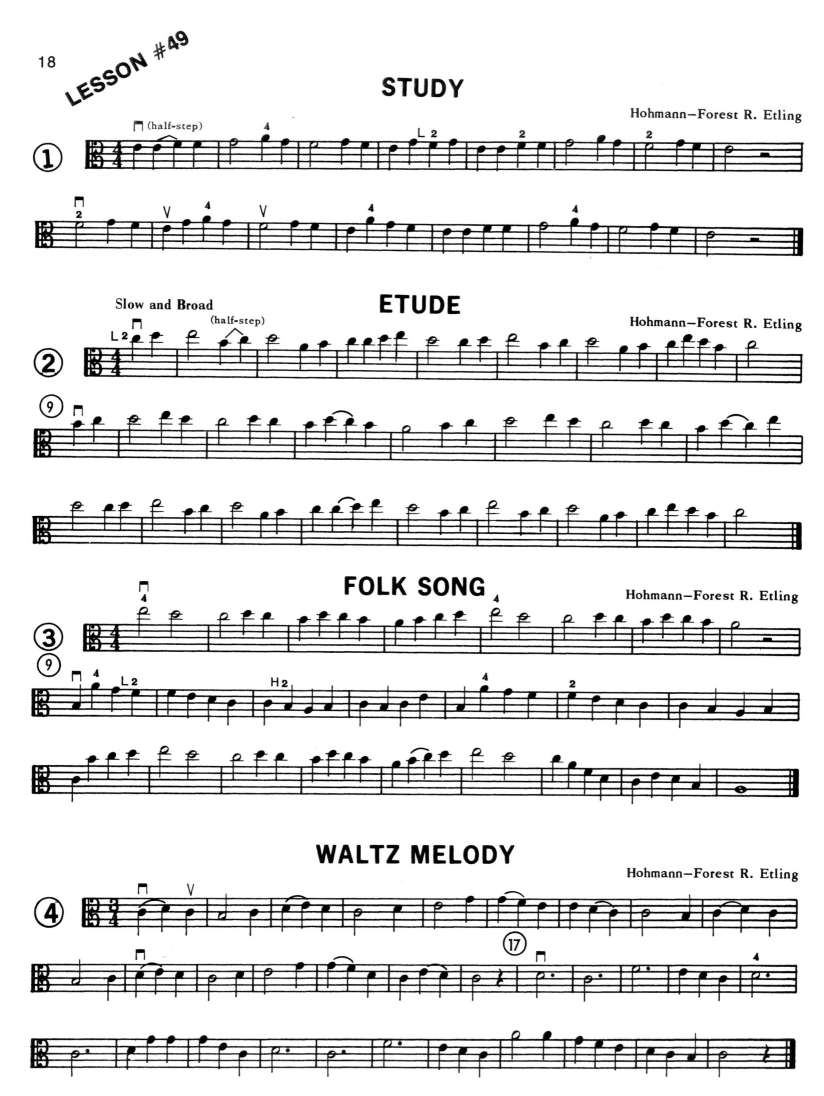

LESSON #50

MERRILY, MERRILY
(4 part round)

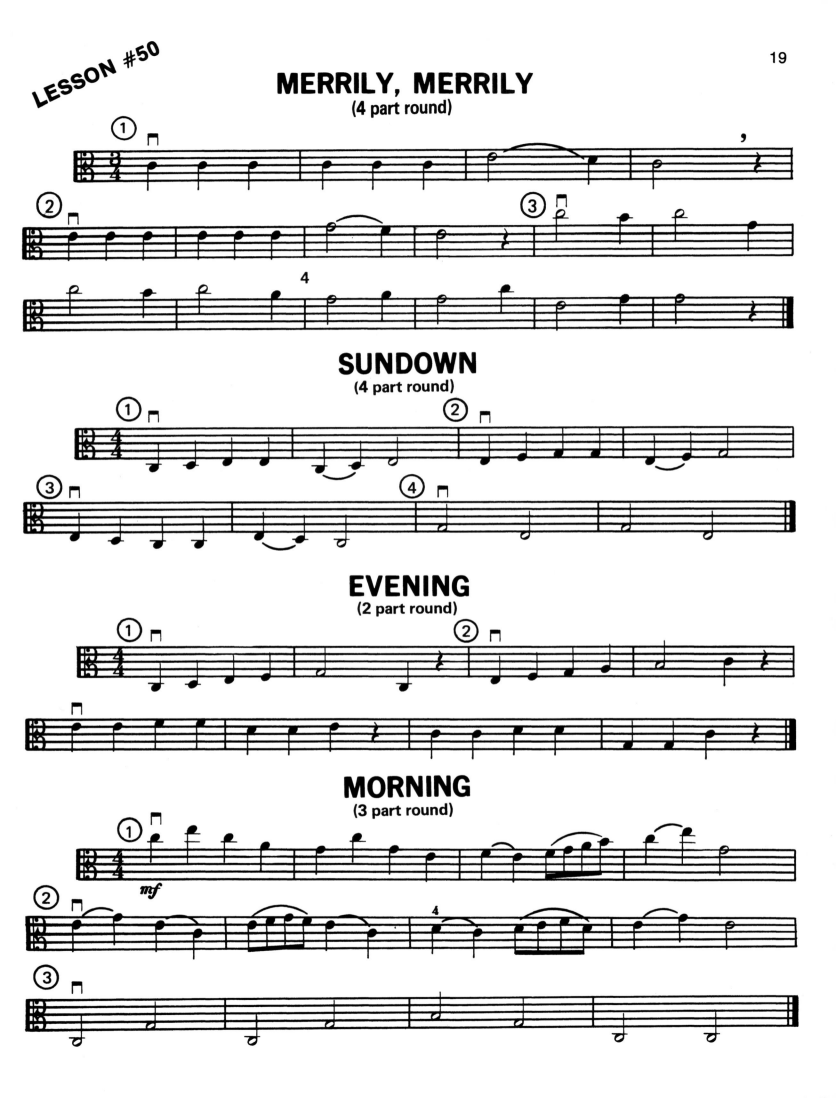

SUNDOWN
(4 part round)

EVENING
(2 part round)

MORNING
(3 part round)

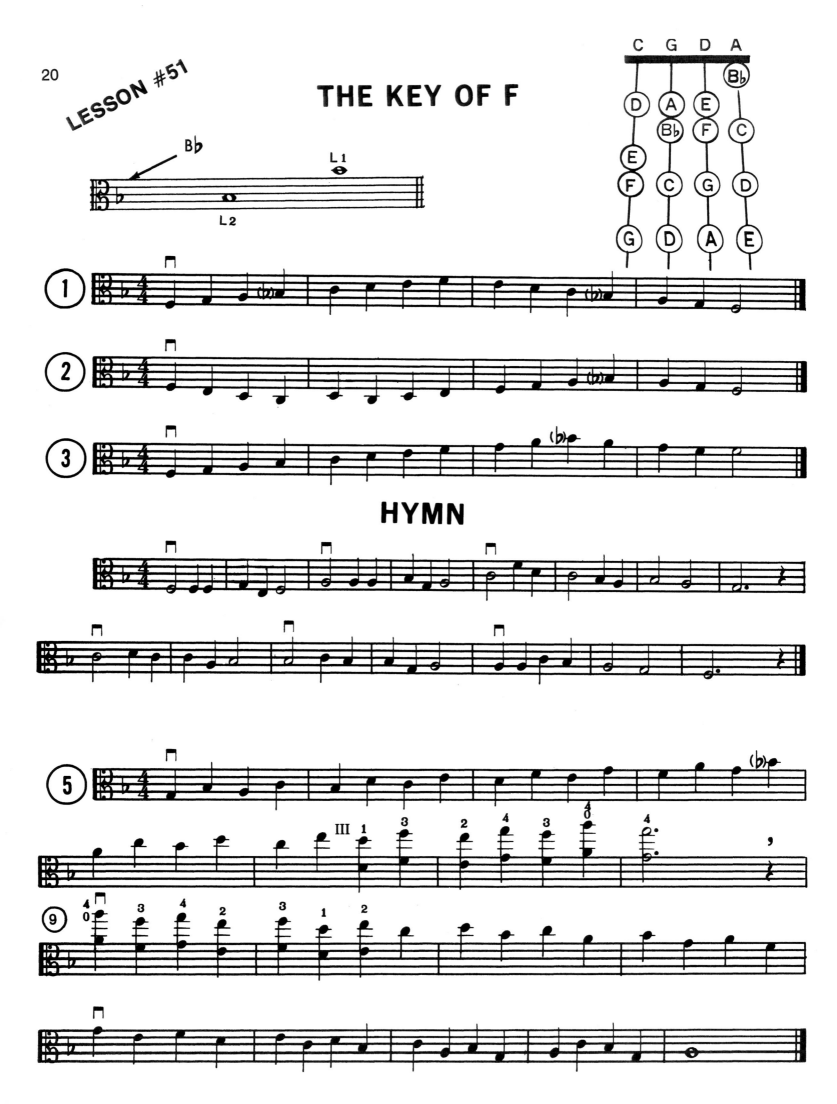

LESSON #52

THEME AND VARIATIONS IN F

LESSON #53

SONG

Slowly

Hohmann—Forest R. Etling

MELODY

Hohmann—Forest R. Etling

TWILIGHT SONG

Hohmann—Forest R. Etling

LESSON #54

THE F SCALE
(2 part round)

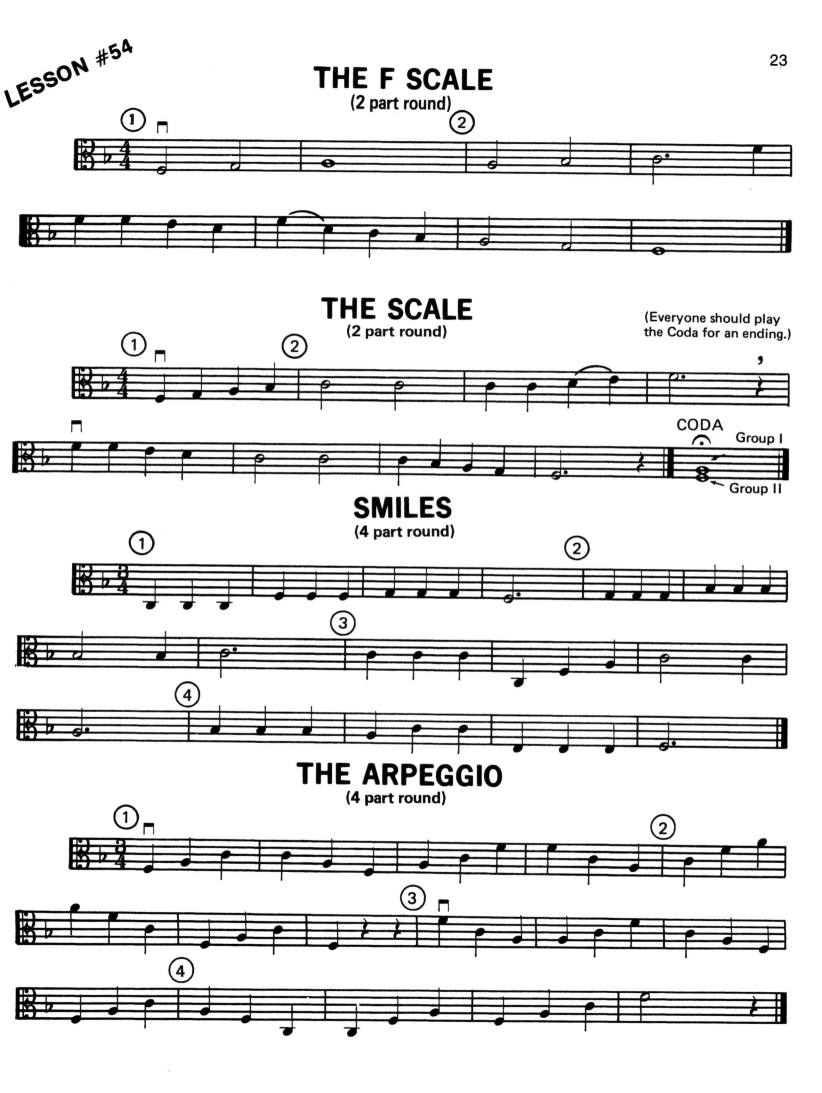

THE SCALE
(2 part round)

(Everyone should play
the Coda for an ending.)

CODA

Group I

Group II

SMILES
(4 part round)

THE ARPEGGIO
(4 part round)

THE DOTTED QUARTER NOTE

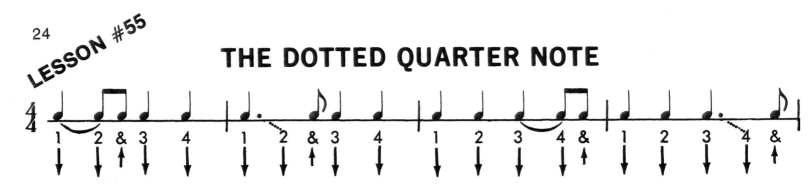

Practice the above by tapping the foot and counting aloud. Pay attention to the position of the foot as each note is counted. Tap your foot "down" on the "beat" and "up" on the "and." You may also clap the hands to indicate the rhythm as you tap the foot and count aloud.

HEROIC MARCH

Handel
arr. by Forest R. Etling

I'VE BEEN WORKIN' ON THE RAILROAD

Folk Song
arr. Forest R. Etling

WAR MARCH OF THE PRIESTS

Mendelssohn
arr. Forest R. Etling

THE BARBER OF SEVILLE

Rossini
arr. Forest R. Etling

LESSON #56

NATURAL HARMONICS

To produce a natural harmonic, extend the fourth finger forward to the middle of the string. Do NOT press the finger down. $\frac{4}{0}$ = natural harmonic

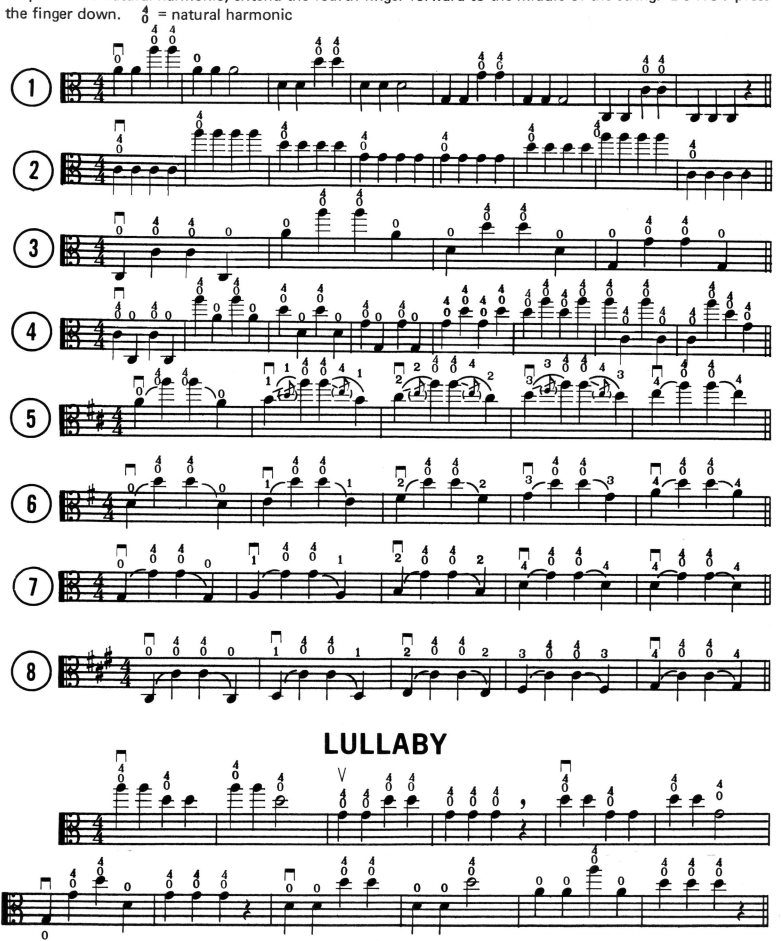

LULLABY

THE G SCALE

THE C SCALE

FRENCH SONG

BENEATH THY GUIDING HAND

THE CLOWN

Preparation

NEW NOTES FOR THE CELLOS

DANISH FOLK SONG

THANKSGIVING SONG

THE MINSTREL BOY

FASCINATION

MARCHETTI
arr. by Forest R. Etling

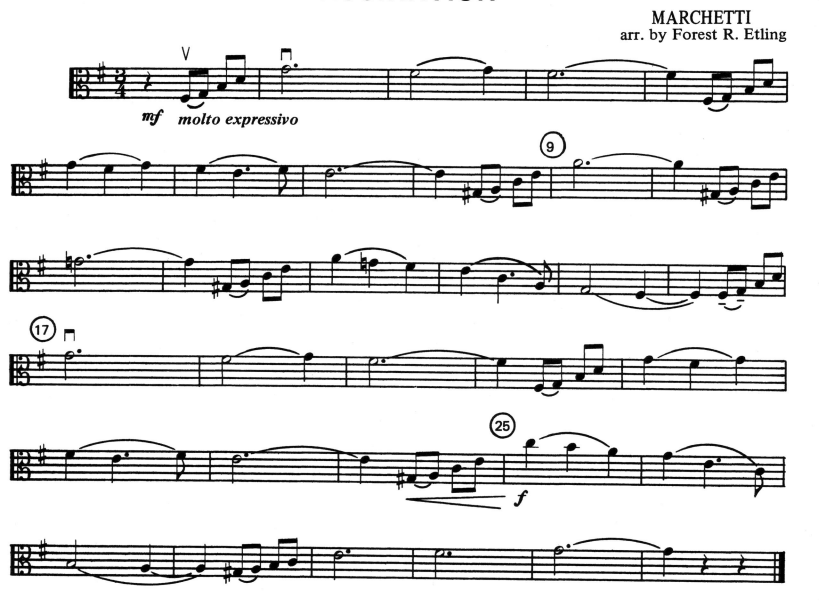

BLUE BELLS OF SCOTLAND

NEW NOTES AND NEW FINGERINGS

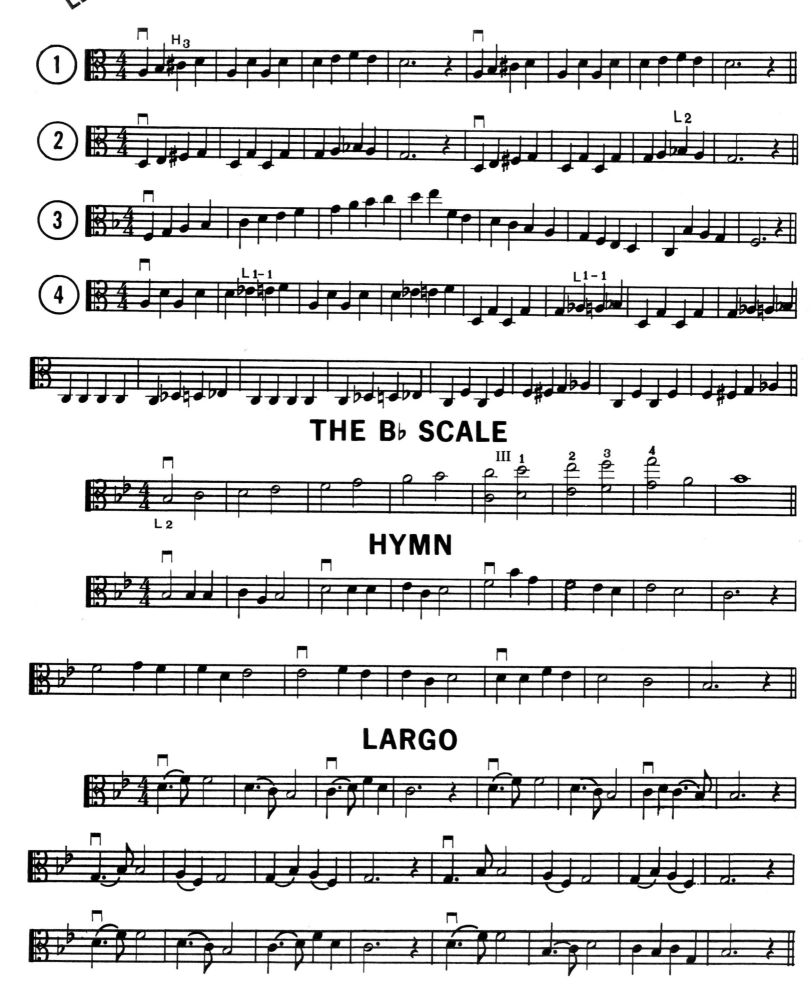

THE B♭ SCALE

HYMN

LARGO

LESSON #60

ISRAELI SONGS

RELIGIOSO

BENEATH THY GUIDING HAND

CRUSADERS' HYMN

ONWARD CHRISTIAN SOLDIERS